Mental Illness and Homelessness

John Allen

San Diego, CA

About the Author
John Allen is a writer who lives in Oklahoma City.

© 2025 ReferencePoint Press, Inc.
Printed in the United States

For more information, contact:
ReferencePoint Press, Inc.
PO Box 27779
San Diego, CA 92198
www.ReferencePointPress.com

ALL RIGHTS RESERVED.
No part of this work covered by the copyright hereon may be reproduced or used in any form or by any means—graphic, electronic, or mechanical, including photocopying, recording, taping, web distribution, or information storage retrieval systems—without the written permission of the publisher.

Picture Credits:

Cover: KT Gravatt/Shutterstock.com

6: Leonard Zhukovsky/Shutterstock.com
10: Hum Historical/Alamy Stock Photo
12: PictureLux/The Hollywood Archive/Alamy Stock Photo
16: Tunatura/Shutterstock.com
20: Monkey Business Images/Shutterstock.com
22: Monkey Business Images/Shutterstock.com

25: Associated Press
30: Liz Albro Photography/Shutterstock.com
33: Sarah Reingewirtz/ZUMAPRESS/Newscom
39: Sheila Fitzgerald/Shutterstock.com
42: Dragana Gordic/Shutterstock.com
44: Ron Adar/ZUMAPRESS/Newscom
48: Associated Press
50: Consolidated News Photos/Shutterstock.com
52: Eduardo Sverdlin/UPI/Newscom

LIBRARY OF CONGRESS CATALOGING-IN-PUBLICATION DATA

Names: Allen, John, 1957- author.
Title: Mental illness and homelessness / by John Allen.
Description: San Diego, CA : ReferencePoint Press, Inc., 2025. | Includes bibliographical references and index.
Identifiers: LCCN 2024013331 (print) | LCCN 2024013332 (ebook) | ISBN 9781678208080 (library binding) | ISBN 9781678208097 (ebook)
Subjects: LCSH: Mentally ill homeless persons--United States--Juvenile literature.
Classification: LCC HV3006.A4 A46 2025 (print) | LCC HV3006.A4 (ebook) | DDC 362.30973--dc23/eng/20240416
LC record available at https://lccn.loc.gov/2024013331
LC ebook record available at https://lccn.loc.gov/2024013332

CONTENTS

Introduction 4
A Controversial Policy on the Mentally Ill Homeless

Chapter One 8
A Problem with No Easy Solutions

Chapter Two 18
Challenges Faced by Mentally Ill Homeless People

Chapter Three 28
Laws Affecting Homeless People with Mental Illness

Chapter Four 37
Getting Necessary Medication

Chapter Five 46
Working Toward Solutions

Source Notes	55
For Further Research	59
Index	62

INTRODUCTION

A Controversial Policy on the Mentally Ill Homeless

In late November 2023, New York City mayor Eric Adams announced a breakthrough in the city's efforts to deal with rising homelessness. He said that during the preceding year, fifty-four people with severe mental illness had been moved off the streets and into stable housing or treatment centers. This group included those who were hardest to reach and resistant to psychiatric care. City officials were hopeful the effort would help these individuals stabilize their lives.

Adams was touting a controversial policy he implemented to deal with New Yorkers who are both homeless and mentally ill. Under the directive, first responders and outreach workers were trained and authorized to provide care for homeless people showing signs of serious mental illness. They sought people who were unable to meet their own needs or had become a danger to themselves or others. Those identified as problem cases were forcibly removed to mental health shelters or other housing. The city has spent more than $1 billion creating these shelters, where psychiatrists meet with homeless patients and provide support.

Clinical experts on homelessness objected that the plan did not address the root causes of the problem, such as addiction and lack of affordable housing. Some warned that forced uprooting of the homeless could cause more harm than good. But Adams saw the early results as a positive first step. "We acknowledge our moral obligation to help them get the treatment and the care they need," he said, "and we're not going to pretend anything other than that is acceptable."[1]

A Problem That Continues to Grow

Cities large and small across the nation are facing the combined problems of homelessness and mental illness. According to data from the US Department of Housing and Urban Development (HUD), there were more than 122,000 homeless people with severe mental illness in 2022. This represents about 21 percent of the 582,000 Americans who experienced homelessness that year. And the problem continues to grow. A landmark 2023 study by researchers at the University of California, San Francisco (UCSF), found that nearly 50 percent of the homeless in California suffer from some form of mental illness, including depression, anxiety, and addiction. Twelve percent reported having frequent hallucinations. These conditions naturally lead to other problems on the streets. Subjects in the UCSF study reported frequent run-ins with the police, with more than 33 percent having spent at least one night in jail.

> "We acknowledge our moral obligation to help [the homeless mentally ill] get the treatment and the care they need, and we're not going to pretend anything other than that is acceptable."[1]
>
> —Eric Adams, mayor of New York City

The UCSF study also showed how quickly people suffering from mental illness can descend into homelessness. Many reported that they had little notice—a median of about ten days—before losing their homes. Those depending on the patience and generosity of family or friends could find themselves out on the street even more suddenly, without even an eviction notice, should that patience wear out. Most of the mentally ill homeless said that a subsidy of a few hundred dollars a month could have kept them from losing their homes.

Facing a Public Backlash

The problem of homelessness among those with mental illness is related to a long-term effort to remove patients from state mental

Cities large and small across the nation are facing the combined problems of homelessness and mental illness. According to data from the US Department of Housing and Urban Development, there were more than 122,000 homeless people with severe mental illness in 2022.

hospitals. Experts in mental health came to view these facilities as cruel environments where people were locked away against their will. But the successful effort to release patients has not been accompanied by an adequate system of treatment and support in the community. Too often, unsupervised patients either do not receive or fail to take medications they need to control their mental illness. Many turn instead to street drugs to calm their shattered nerves. This can result in erratic behavior, with individuals endangering themselves and others.

In 2018, a federal court ruled that cities could not prevent homeless people from living in public spaces. Partly as a result, encampments of the homeless have sprouted in cities across the nation, raising concerns among citizens about safety, sanitation, and public order. The public backlash has produced a storm of complaints. According to a 2019 study by the *American Sociological Review*, San Francisco saw its number of 911 emergency calls about homeless-related problems increase by 72 percent. And 311 calls complaining about nonemergency situations soared by 781 percent. John Brownstein, an epidemiologist at Boston Children's Hospital and an expert on public health surveillance, says the homeless and mentally ill are now more visible, which leads to the backlash. "While annual HUD statistics are informative," says Brownstein, "the alarming increase in civic complaints in cities like San Francisco, not linked to criminal activities but rather societal concerns, accentuates the heightened visibility of this challenge."[2]

A Possible Solution in Outreach

Amid growing criticism, city officials are finding there are no easy answers to the plight of the homeless and mentally ill. In November 2023, San Francisco began to clear away homeless encampments in preparation for an international economic conference, but the city's efforts were eventually blocked by a federal judge. Forcible removal, like Mayor Adams's program in New York City, also faces opposition among experts. A better approach, they say, is to dispatch outreach teams to locate and engage with homeless people. By building trust through personal relationships, these teams can convince the homeless to move into shelters and accept treatment. Shayan Rab, a psychiatrist working with the Los Angeles County Department of Mental Health, stresses the need to be relentless in outreach. "Every once in a while, people in interim housing, they make a rapid turn," says Rab. "The bond with the team gets better. They start trusting us. . . . We are showing up every day because, you know, we know that homelessness . . . can result in an early death."[3]

> "The bond with the team gets better. They start trusting us. . . . We are showing up every day because, you know, we know that homelessness . . . can result in an early death."[3]
>
> —Shayan Rab, a psychiatrist who works with the Los Angeles County Department of Mental Health

CHAPTER ONE

A Problem with No Easy Solutions

Mental illness that leads to homelessness can afflict people of all kinds. Jo Franklin was a television journalist and award-winning documentary filmmaker whose focus was the turbulent Middle East. In 2014, the University of Florida, Franklin's alma mater, planned to honor her at a Washington, DC, gala. But the event fell apart due to unforeseen problems. A $2 million donation Franklin had pledged to the university proved to be a mirage when her check bounced. Her reservation at a luxury DC hotel was canceled due to a rejected credit card. Sixty-eight-year-old Franklin became estranged from her daughter and other family members, and her life fell into disarray.

In subsequent years, she frequently met for coffee with a group of young admirers in Palm Beach Gardens, Florida. Franklin often seemed paranoid, telling her friends that she did not carry a cellphone because dangerous people from Saudi Arabia were trying to track her movements. She claimed to have access to a private jet and to be friends with Great Britain's Prince Harry. Yet her coffee group noticed that she wore the same clothes for weeks at a time, including worn-out sandals.

It turned out that she was sleeping in a parking garage and had been arrested several times for drug possession and stealing boxes of wine. Depressed from a traumatic divorce and suffering from delusions, Franklin had spiraled downward into homelessness. She died in July 2023, having reconciled at last with her family. "She hurt so many people," said her son, Hugh

Trout. But he added, "Nobody was more of a victim of whatever this illness was than herself."[4]

Finding Humane Alternatives for Mental Health Care

Franklin's story shows the challenges of dealing with mental illness that leads to homelessness. Despite her family's repeated attempts to get clinical help for her, she refused to admit she had a problem and rejected all offers of treatment. The more others tried, the more she lied and withdrew into her delusions. "When anyone started to tamper with that fantasyland, it would get very, very dark," said Trout. "My hope is just there was a way, even if she didn't want it, to be forced to sit down with a mental health professional and figure out, 'What is there to do here?'"[5]

Decades ago, someone like Franklin might have been legally committed to a mental hospital. During the mid-1950s, more than half a million people were housed in state psychiatric hospitals—or asylums, as they were often called. As the number of patients grew, facilities could not keep up with their needs. Hospitals were understaffed and lacked sufficient accommodations to provide proper care. Patient conditions resembled the harsh treatment found in prisons and jails. Steven Sharfstein, the former president of the American Psychiatric Association, recalls the atmosphere at the Boston State Hospital in Mattapan, Massachusetts, a creaking hulk built during the nineteenth century. "It was a terrible place," says Sharfstein. "The lights didn't always work, the patients wandered around like zombies. Nobody got better."[6]

> "[Boston State Hospital] was a terrible place. The lights didn't always work, the patients wandered around like zombies. Nobody got better."[6]
>
> —Steven Sharfstein, former president of the American Psychiatric Association

Social critics called for an overhaul of the state-run systems. Public attitudes about mental health and the rights of patients also began to change. States felt pressure to find humane alternatives to the prison-like institutions. At the same time, a new factor appeared to offer hope for the treatment of mental illness.

In 1954, the Food, Drug, and Insecticide Administration approved an antipsychotic drug with the trade name Thorazine. It was first used as a preanesthetic agent for surgery, serving to make patients calmer without losing consciousness. Thorazine showed promise in treating mental illnesses, including schizophrenia and bipolar disorder. Some experts suggested that this breakthrough in medication could make inpatient psychiatric hospitals obsolete.

Rejecting Outdated Mental Institutions

As a result of new attitudes and new medications, national mental health policy changed to embrace deinstitutionalization. The idea was to remove patients from state hospitals and place them into community mental health centers where they could receive support and more personal care. It was hoped that patients would ultimately be able to live on their own. A 1965 law that created Medicaid, a national health care program for low-income Americans, forbade federal payment for care in state psychiatric hospitals, which also hastened their demise. It seemed that a new, more humane approach to mental illness was at hand.

Decades ago, the mentally ill were housed in state psychiatric hospitals, like the Government Hospital for the Insane (pictured), in Washington, DC. Patient conditions resembled the harsh treatment found in prisons and jails.

When Prisons Serve as Mental Facilities

The movement to shut down harsh and outdated state psychiatric hospitals during the 1950s left many patients with nowhere to go. Over the years, some turned to life in cheap tenements or on the streets. As the population of homeless and mentally ill people grew, many more ended up in jails and prisons. Today, say mental health experts, state prisons serve as de facto mental institutions, with large numbers of inmates suffering from severe mental illness. According to the most recent national Survey of Prison Inmates, 56 percent of inmates report a recent or prior history of mental health problems. Yet only 26 percent have received professional psychiatric help since being incarcerated. Only about 6 percent currently get counseling or therapy. The situation for female inmates is even worse, with rates of bipolar disorder and severe depression that are double the rate for males.

In general, prisons are not equipped to handle the growing wave of inmates with mental illness. Alisa Roth, author of *Insane: America's Criminal Treatment of Mental Illness,* observes, "In many prisons and jails, the urgent question is not how to reduce this surging population but how to build larger and better psychiatric units and treatment facilities inside the walls."

Alisa Roth, "The Truth About Deinstitutionalization," *The Atlantic,* May 25, 2021. www.theatlantic.com.

The new policy had a significant impact on mental health care. The number of patients living in state mental hospitals dropped from 535,000 in 1960 to 137,000 in 1980. In California alone, the number of state hospital beds fell from 37,000 in 1955 to 2,500 in 1983. But many of the promised improvements failed to materialize. Due to funding shortfalls, less than half of the facilities outlined in the 1963 Community Mental Health Centers Act were actually built. Thorazine, although helpful for treating schizophrenia and bipolar disorder, was certainly not a cure. Moreover, the drug had serious side effects, such as dizziness, confusion, and even muscle spasms and twitches similar to Parkinson's disease. Efforts to provide medication to the mentally ill lacked a focused plan.

Nonetheless, many patients suddenly found themselves on the streets with limited ability to care for themselves. Increasing numbers fell into homelessness. Studies during the late 1980s found that 27 to 38 percent of patients discharged from state mental hospitals became homeless with no stable address. The limited supply of psychiatric beds continued to shrink, with criminal offenders occupying most of those that remained. Some families found that pressing criminal charges against mentally ill relatives gave them a better chance of getting their loved ones the treatment they needed.

A Further Wave of Deinstitutionalization

Influenced by films like *One Flew Over the Cuckoo's Nest* (1975), which depicted the cruel treatment of mental patients in a state facility, the public continued to see deinstitutionalizing as the most humane option. And there was more to come. In 1981 the administration of President Ronald Reagan repealed a major budgetary act, effectively erasing funding for federal mental health hospitals. This brought another wave of releases, forcing patients either to seek care on the state level or rely on community clinics. Thousands more individuals with severe mental illness ended up homeless and living on the streets. An estimated 50 to 60 percent of those released had been diagnosed with schizophrenia and required medications and psychiatric care. The sight of homeless mentally ill people became more common in cities and towns.

Influenced by films like One Flew Over the Cuckoo's Nest *(pictured), which depicted mistreatment of mentally ill patients, the public continued to see deinstitutionalizing as the most humane option.*

Many psychiatric professionals view the trend as a disastrous failure. Divya Kakaiya began her career as a psychologist during the mid-1980s, with California's movement to deinstitutionalize the mentally ill in full swing. She worries that people with serious mental illness cannot get the medications and therapies they need to even have a chance for meaningful lives. "We need to recognize that deinstitutionalization of the mentally ill is one of the primary causes of the rise of homelessness all over the country," Kakaiya wrote in an April 2023 opinion piece. "Do mentally ill homeless people deserve care, dignity, security, compassion and brain growth? We know the answer is yes."[7]

> "We need to recognize that deinstitutionalization of the mentally ill is one of the primary causes of the rise of homelessness all over the country. Do mentally ill homeless people deserve care, dignity, security, compassion and brain growth? We know the answer is yes."[7]
>
> —Divya Kakaiya, a psychologist and neuroscientist in San Diego, California

Suing for Patients' Civil Rights

The movement to release mental patients from institutions also had roots in the 1960s push for civil rights and civil liberties. Groups such as the American Civil Liberties Union (ACLU) went to court to prevent people with mental illness from being committed to state hospitals against their will. This crusade for patients' rights was candid about its aims. Bruce Ennis, one of the ACLU's top attorneys during the 1960s and 1970s, declared, "My personal goal is either to abolish involuntary commitment or to set up so many procedural roadblocks and hurdles that it will be difficult, if not impossible, for the state to commit people against their will."[8]

Ennis and other lawyers sued states to demand expensive upgrades to mental health facilities. If successful, the suits could force institutions to shut down for lack of funds. Patients might win release, but instead of getting the clinical help they desperately needed, most wound up on the streets to fend for themselves. California set up arbitrary limits of seventeen days for holding mental patients involuntarily, expanded to ninety days for the most severe cases. These limits had no basis in research or

Striking a Blow for Disability Rights

Growing up in a public housing project, Lois Curtis endured violence and poverty throughout her youth. At age twelve, she was diagnosed with schizophrenia and severe mental disabilities. She was ruled unfit for public school and was forced to attend a special center for psychological education. Her traumatic separation from family and friends made her behavior problems even worse. Finally, she ended up in a psychiatric hospital far from her home. Throughout her teens and early twenties, Curtis shuttled endlessly between hospitals and private care facilities, always segregated because of her mental illness and disability.

A social worker introduced Curtis to Sue Jamieson, a lawyer at Atlanta Legal Aid. In 1995, after listening to Curtis's story, Jamieson filed suit against the Georgia Department of Human Resources and its commissioner, Tommy Olmstead. Four years later, the Supreme Court ruled in favor of Curtis and her coplaintiff, a woman named Elaine Wilson. The decision prohibited segregation of people with disabilities, including mental illness. It also furthered the cause of deinstitutionalization. Curtis was able to live on her own and pursue her love of painting. "She never went back to hospital," said Jamieson in 2014. "And Lois has become a respected artist with regular exhibitions of her work."

Sue Jamieson, "The Olmstead Decision and Its Aftermath," *Impact*, vol. 28, no. 1, Winter 2015. https://publications.ici.umn.edu.

---

prior practice. But politicians on all sides found something to like about them, whether because of patients' supposed freedom or the savings in state funds.

In November 1993, a case in Washington, DC, brought the issue to national attention. Yetta Adams, a middle-aged woman suffering from schizophrenia, was found dead at a bus stop across from HUD. At first, the national media focused on the bitter irony of a homeless woman dying outside the nation's agency for housing. HUD secretary Henry G. Cisneros responded with a heartfelt editorial in the *Washington Post*. "The temptation is strong to see Yetta Adams' death as an indictment of a callous, uncaring people, or as a sign that the problem has become so intractable that efforts to help the homeless are doomed to failure," wrote Cisneros. "But indicting each other is too easy. And viewing homelessness as intractable is simply wrong."[9]

But the real story was Adams's lack of mental health care. Due to the voices swirling in her head from her brain disorder, she struggled to take care of herself. She lacked access to medications for managing her schizophrenia. She also failed to take the insulin she needed to control her diabetes, which contributed to her death. Some psychiatric experts argued that people like Adams with severe mental illness suffered unnecessarily from current mental health policies. These policies prevented them from being forcibly committed and getting the personal care that could save their lives. In addition, research showed the dangers of such neglect. Left untreated, schizophrenia could lead to a major psychotic break, thus reducing the possibility of future recovery and causing permanent damage.

Struggling to Implement the *Olmstead* Decision

The 2000s saw the numbers of homeless with mental illness rise across the nation. Courts continued to favor patients' rights over their need for mandatory care. In 1999, the Supreme Court ruled in *Olmstead v. LC* that placing people with mental illness in mental health hospitals against their will violated the Americans with Disabilities Act and discriminated against them illegally. Instead, states were required to provide services that would help to integrate patients into the community. Questions of how to fund and operate these community centers were left to states and cities. The decision set off a new wave of lawsuits against outdated mental health facilities and triggered more patient releases. Many of the lawsuits were filed by federal agencies. Once more, deinstitutionalization left many patients with severe mental illness homeless and without resources or access to care.

Implementing programs based on *Olmstead* became a priority in Washington, DC. In 2001, President George W. Bush announced the New Freedom Initiative to remove barriers to community living for people with disabilities, including those with mental illness. In 2009, the ten-year anniversary of the *Olmstead* decision, President Barack Obama launched a program called the Year of Community Living to emphasize civil rights for people with disabilities. Obama's Department of Justice made a point of promoting *Olmstead* enforcement across the nation.

Some experts argue that people with severe mental illness suffer unnecessarily from current mental health policies, which prevent them from being forcibly committed and getting proper care.

But states have struggled to meet the goals and timelines set out in *Olmstead*. Not enough community housing and care facilities have been built to stem the tide of homelessness among the mentally ill. Funding from Medicaid, the federal health insurance program for low-income Americans, generally has proved inadequate to comply with the *Olmstead* requirements and patients' needs. On the twenty-fourth anniversary of the landmark ruling, the administration of President Joe Biden admitted the shortcomings while stressing its ongoing commitment to *Olmstead*'s goals. "The *Olmstead* decision transformed federal and state policy from a segregated, institutional service model to promote community-based supports," said Melanie Fontes Rainer, director of the Office for Civil Rights at the Department of Health and Human Services. "Yet, we acknowledge that for many, the promise of *Olmstead* is still unfulfilled, as some people with disabilities continue to spend their lives in institutions or at risk of being institutionalized without sufficient access to alternatives."[10]

Humane Intentions and Unintentional Consequences

Recent government research shows that the plight of the mentally ill homeless remains a national problem. A 2022 survey by HUD found that there were about 580,000 homeless people in the United States, of which nearly 250,000 suffer from some form of mental illness. HUD estimated that at least 100,000 suffer from severe mental illness, and many mental health experts say the actual number is likely much higher. And the problem is getting worse, with the number of homeless in 2023 rising by more than 70,000, or 12 percent, with a similar spike in the number of mentally ill homeless.

The movement to rescue those with serious mental illness from outdated state facilities, which dates back to the 1960s, began with humane intentions. However, it has sparked a backlash among clinical experts and the public alike due to unintentional consequences. "Since the earliest days of deinstitutionalization, the number of psychiatric hospital beds in America has declined relentlessly, so that it is rarely possible to treat the full episode of illness in hospital," says Harold I. Schwartz, chief psychiatrist at Hartford Hospital's Institute of Living. "Despite all the talk and the intermittent media coverage, our attention spans are short. . . . We seem to be OK with the homeless mentally ill wandering the streets."[11]

> "Despite all the talk and the intermittent media coverage, our attention spans are short. . . . We seem to be OK with the homeless mentally ill wandering the streets."[11]
>
> —Harold I. Schwartz, chief psychiatrist at Hartford Hospital's Institute of Living

17

CHAPTER TWO

Challenges Faced by Mentally Ill Homeless People

John, a homeless man in Gainesville, Florida, shares the daily problems faced by thousands of people who live on the streets. These include obtaining nutritious food, finding transportation, and struggling to keep a few possessions. But John's serious mental illness makes everything more difficult. When outreach workers from Gainesville's Helping Hands Clinic (HHC) approached John and offered him assistance, he reacted with paranoia and erratic behavior. The workers persisted, however, until they felt they had made a connection with John and gained his trust.

But his psychosis nearly derailed the process. "When we attempted a second meeting with John, it was as if they had not met before," reports the HHC on its website. And simply getting him to the clinic, which is staffed with social workers, physicians, and nurse practitioners, was a major challenge. HHC goes on to observe:

> We also invited John to visit Helping Hands' Monday night clinic for a meal and access to a clothing closet. In the big picture, though, getting to the clinic would involve taking a bus that stops three times before it reaches HHC, and a round trip could take approximately five hours to complete. . . . Added to that, for him, are problems related to homelessness in general. Having strong body odor, feeling invisible, and being abused by people he might encounter, are just a few of them.[12]

A Struggle to Survive

For the homeless with mental illness, every day is a struggle to survive. Homelessness is already linked with a greater than normal risk of death from many causes, including infectious diseases, heart disease, cancer, substance abuse, and accidental injury. For the mentally ill homeless, suicide is another major risk. In 2020, the *Psychiatric Times* reported that in a large sample of homeless adults, nearly 8 percent had attempted suicide within the past thirty days. People who are homeless and mentally ill face a constant challenge merely to take care of their basic needs, such as adequate food, water, and protection from the elements. Their psychiatric needs often are not a priority unless a crisis forces the issue.

> "In the big picture, though, getting to the clinic would involve taking a bus that stops three times before it reaches HHC. . . . Added to that, for [John], are problems related to homelessness in general. Having strong body odor, feeling invisible, and being abused by people he might encounter, are just a few of them."[12]
>
> —Helping Hands Clinic in Gainesville, Florida

The state of being homeless also can help trigger some kinds of mental disorders. Homeless people can suffer from anxiety, depression, paranoia, trauma, and anhedonia, which is the inability to experience joy or pleasure. These conditions can drain away any motivation for seeking psychiatric care, even when it is desperately needed. The anxiety and stress can become like a crushing weight. "It took a real turn for my mental health," says Janet Smith, who escaped the cycle of homelessness with the aid of Breaktime, an outreach group for homeless young people in Boston. "I felt that nobody wanted to help me, nobody wanted to do anything for me. I didn't want to do anything for myself."[13]

Lack of transportation is a constant concern. It makes it difficult for the homeless to keep mental health appointments, obtain medications, or tend to other medical needs. Public transportation presents more problems, as with John in Gainesville. Bus lines or streetcars may not exist, may be limited in their routes, or have haphazard service. Often, people living on the streets lack money for fares. Figuring out how to get somewhere can seem like a monumental task.

Practical considerations that others take for granted can fall into a chaotic jumble. Even if the homeless mentally ill make it to a hospital or clinic, they need help accessing government resources that could pay for treatment, such as Medicaid or the Affordable Care Act. They may not even be aware such resources are available. Lack of a mailing address or bank account prevents them from applying for housing or other kinds of benefits. Perhaps surprisingly, homeless persons are likely to have a mobile phone; according to research at the University of Southern California's Price School of Public Policy, more than 94 percent do. But they struggle to keep the phone charged or keep from losing it due to neglect or theft. Their ability to receive text alerts about medical appointments or opportunities for care is limited. Internet use may be restricted to occasional visits to the public library.

There is also the perpetual stigma attached to homeless individuals with mental illness. They lose connection with the people around them and become social outcasts. They wear the same clothes for weeks on end and lack the means to bathe, brush their teeth, or get a haircut. Passersby avoid them instinctively.

Homeless people face obstacles every day. These include obtaining nutritious food, finding transportation, and struggling to keep a few possessions. Sometimes they are able to find outreach programs that can help.

Finding a Job While Homeless

Simply applying for a job can become an intricate hassle for the homeless. Vivien, a fifty-one-year-old woman who worked full-time as a delivery truck driver, lost her job due to complications from COVID-19. In 2022, she had been unhoused for three months and living at the Central Arizona Shelter Services homeless shelter. Vivien was eager to seek work, but her situation kept throwing roadblocks in her way. Her lack of a laptop computer and reliable Wi-Fi made it hard to apply for jobs. With no data plan and limited minutes, her smartphone seemed much less smart than usual. Moreover, job-finding websites were filled with pop-up features and boxed videos that made her phone seize up.

Vivien increasingly felt the mental burden of depression and anxiety for the future. She swore that things were simpler during a previous short stint in prison rather than in her homeless predicament. "In prison I could ask someone to help me find work after, I could use computers to find something for when I got out," she says. "Here, we are just on our own. Any issue I face, any hardship, I have to face it alone."

Quoted in Natalie Florence and Heather Ross, "How Tech Can Make It Excruciatingly Hard to Apply for a Job While Homeless," *Slate*, June 27, 2023. www.slate.com.

Run-ins with law enforcement tend to make them feel even more paranoid and isolated. "You don't feel important anymore," says Smith. "You don't feel like you're part of society. You don't feel like you're a part of anything. You feel like you're being looked down on. . . . You can hear people mumbling, talking . . . they give a disgusted look. That right there can bring anybody down . . . [it] is 100% just crushing."[14]

The Vicious Cycle of Homelessness

Mental illness is one of the root causes of homelessness, along with job loss, substance abuse, and lack of affordable housing. When people become homeless, they may think it is only a temporary setback. Some do manage to bounce back and find stable housing relatively quickly. But escaping the vicious cycle of homelessness can be extremely difficult. This is especially true when an individual has a severe mental illness, such as schizophrenia, bipolar disorder, or chronic depression. It can be nearly impossible for them to hold a job and thus keep up with financial responsibilities.

Escaping the vicious cycle of homelessness can be extremely difficult. Some people are lucky enough to find temporary housing in shelters.

Many people are shocked at how quickly their problems can snowball, leaving them unable to keep up with mortgage payments or rent. What seems at first to be a temporary circumstance can slide into a long-term cycle of confusion, pain, victimhood, physical and mental decline, and dependency on handouts. The struggle to return to a normal life can finally seem all but futile.

Traumatic events such as losing a job or getting divorced can also trigger the symptoms of mental illness, including stress, anxiety, and depression. Becoming homeless only makes these symptoms worse. A landmark study of the homeless in California between October 2021 and November 2022 revealed how people can become locked into a cycle of despair. The California Statewide Study of People Experiencing Homelessness (CASPEH), conducted by the Benioff Homelessness and Housing Initiative at UCSF, found that nearly half of the respondents had experienced symptoms of depression or anxiety. Twelve percent suffered from hallucinations. About 33 percent had spent at least one night in jail during their latest bout of homelessness.

22

For most, living on the streets was nothing new. More than 60 percent had been homeless before, with an average stint of twenty-two months. Barely 25 percent had received any kind of monthly assistance. And the day-to-day hazards of their situation added to their stress. At least 75 percent of respondents had experienced physical violence while homeless, and nearly 25 percent had been sexually assaulted.

To deal with the daily trauma, people living on the streets often turn to drugs and alcohol. Nearly one in three of the CASPEH respondents, many with diagnosed mental illness, had taken methamphetamine. "People talked to us really plainly about how they couldn't possibly stop using drugs until they were housed," says Margot Kushel, who led the study. "Many were using drugs to stay awake, because they were scared of violence if they fell asleep, or their stuff being taken away again. And if you can't fall asleep and you're hungry, then yeah, meth can help you."[15]

> "People talked to us really plainly about how they couldn't possibly stop using drugs until they were housed. Many were using drugs to stay awake, because they were scared of violence if they fell asleep, or their stuff being taken away again. And if you can't fall asleep and you're hungry, then yeah, meth can help you."[15]
>
> —Margot Kushel, director of the California Statewide Study of People Experiencing Homelessness

Poverty and Mental Illness: A Two-Way Street

Researchers note that poverty and mental illness often have a two-way relationship in which one can easily lead to the other. A cursory look at tent encampments in large cities shows how mental illness can lead to poverty and homelessness. But poverty is also the source of many problems with mental health. According to the National Association of Mental Illness (NAMI), those who live in neighborhoods with high rates of poverty tend to have mental health outcomes that are markedly worse than people in low-poverty areas. The outcomes hold true for both children and adults.

Poverty, along with substance abuse and stress, can cause incipient mental illness to develop into a lifelong and lethal condition. One of poverty's most insidious effects is the psychological strain it places on people day after day without letup. Too much of their cognitive capacity is taken up with worries about food insecurity, mounting bills, and unstable housing. Moreover, NAMI has found that Hispanic and African American populations are at even greater risk of serious mental health problems due to social and economic disadvantage. Hispanic people are three times more likely than white people to dwell in high-poverty areas, and Black people are five times more likely. "Certainly, dwelling in the stressful state of poverty can worsen mental illness or ignite it," states the Crisis Assistance Ministry of Charlotte, North Carolina, on its website. "The instability that often accompanies mental illness can also lead to poverty on its own. . . . Being born into a lower-income zip [code] which lacks accessible, affordable, and/or quality resources often means your income will remain lower and your economic mobility limited. This can have negative impacts on mental health."[16]

Living with Serious Mental Illness

Although some homeless people suffer from the reality of poverty, others succumb to delusions and paranoia. Severe mental illnesses, such as schizophrenia and bipolar disorder, when untreated, leave those afflicted in a jumbled state where nothing is quite what it seems. When Diana Grippo first started hearing voices, she was twenty-five—the typical age for the onset of bipolar disorder. She had just earned a degree in economics from the University of California, Los Angeles, with a bright future seemingly in store for her as a teacher.

Instead, she stopped sleeping for days on end. She began to act impulsively, spending her money recklessly and even giving it away. She rejected help from her family and soon ended up living on the streets of San Francisco in the treacherous Tenderloin district. Her manic episodes made her easy prey for violence, and she somehow managed to survive a vicious sexual assault. As Grippo recalls,

In my state of mind, I concentrated on the anger I felt at [the attackers] for having taken my boots. I was livid, and this kept me from being as traumatized as I might have been. I got picked up by the police for walking barefoot on the freeway. The painted lines were softer on my soles. They brought me to a psych ward on a "5150"—the police term for admitting someone to the hospital. I went in and out of hospitals and was misdiagnosed as schizophrenic and given the wrong drugs. Several years later, I was diagnosed as manic-depressive (that's what they called it back then). I was given lithium and it stabilized me for many years. It got rid of the manic episodes, but I was still in a depressive state.[17]

Medication helped Grippo leave the streets and put her life in order. Despite persistent bouts with depression, she began a successful career in sales at Apple. Love and support from family and friends have kept her from becoming just another statistic—a suicide or a victim of murderous violence.

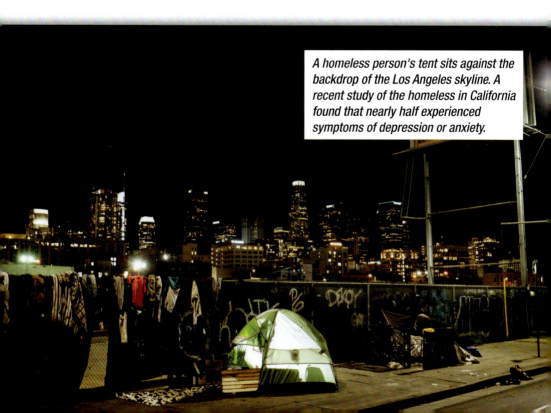

A homeless person's tent sits against the backdrop of the Los Angeles skyline. A recent study of the homeless in California found that nearly half experienced symptoms of depression or anxiety.

Dealing with Trauma and Homelessness

Finding oneself homeless and alone can inflict a crushing trauma. However, psychiatric professionals note that many homeless patients end up on the streets because of traumatic episodes in their past. Ms. Harris, a woman of middle age, has a history of post-traumatic stress disorder (PTSD) that led to problems with alcohol. Her uncle sexually assaulted her when she was twelve, after which her mother swore her to silence about the incident. Harris dropped out of school at age sixteen. At nineteen, she married a man who was physically abusive. She relieved her stress with alcohol for years, and her drinking only became worse after her divorce. Relations with her two children grew strained as Harris used up her finances and landed in a homeless shelter.

When Harris finally entered a substance abuse rehabilitation program, her analyst learned the many reasons for her PTSD and alcoholism, including distrust of others. "In emergency rooms, rates of substance use were significantly higher, sometimes doubled, in homeless patients as compared to those who did not report homelessness," says Dr. Julie Williams, a psychiatrist who specializes in care for the homeless. "While there are many hypotheses surrounding these findings, one cannot ignore the influence of trauma."

Julie Williams, "'I Have No One': Understanding Homelessness and Trauma," *Psychiatric Times*, September 1, 2022. www.psychiatrictimes.com.

Bethany Yeiser survived her own harrowing experience with severe mental illness. In her case, schizophrenia and recurring delusions made her paranoid and caused her to separate from family members and longtime friends. She began sleeping first in a churchyard and later in a university library. An encounter with two kindly Chinese women on a trip to New Mexico convinced her, in her delusional state, that she was destined to be a great spiritual leader in China. She refused to go back to her parents and rejected the antipsychotic medication she needed. Instead, she moved back to the homeless encampments of Los Angeles. It took a determined psychiatrist to get her the treatment that finally saved her. Yeiser says,

> "While onlookers may have seen me living outside, and perhaps judged me, and questioned why I could not work, I wonder if anyone ever thought about what should be done to help me build a new life."[18]
>
> —Bethany Yeiser, a survivor of severe mental illness

Due to the symptoms of my brain disorder, including delusions (fixed false beliefs) and hallucinations, even a very low-stress job was impossible. I think it is probable that many people who saw me living outside assumed I was lazy and/or a drug addict. In fact, I was neither. . . . But while onlookers may have seen me living outside, and perhaps judged me, and questioned why I could not work, I wonder if anyone ever thought about what should be done to help me build a new life.[18]

"Fighting a Fight Every Day"

People who are homeless and mentally ill face daily challenges in trying to survive on the streets. Their struggles are made more difficult by poverty, disease, and neglect. "I am fighting a fight every day," says Janet Smith, who has battled mental illness and homelessness for years. "I fight it every day because it catches up with me every day, but I'm glad that I didn't let it control me."[19]

CHAPTER THREE

Laws Affecting Homeless People with Mental Illness

After a long walk on the streets of Manhattan, tourists and other strollers are likely to search for a hospitable park bench to rest. However, benches in the city are anything but welcoming. Most have been fitted with armrests in the middle, making it uncomfortable to spread out and relax. The borders of public gardens are lined with triangular spikes to discourage stretching out on the grass. The targets of these features are not ordinary pedestrians but rather the city's homeless population. The idea is to prevent individuals living on the streets from sleeping or loitering in public spaces. Advocates for the homeless call these features hostile architecture.

Smaller cities and towns have also adopted this strategy to keep public areas cleared of homeless sleepers. In 2019, administrators in Iowa City, Iowa, drew fire for replacing benches in a pedestrian mall with ones that have thick steel armrests in the middle. The city spent more than $150,000 installing the new benches, money that advocates claimed could have been better spent on shelters and medical treatment for the mentally ill.

In 2023, the National Coalition for the Homeless (NCH) highlighted the issue by publishing an online report titled *Design Against Humanity: Examining Anti-Homeless Architecture*. The report includes photos of benches with intrusive armrests, curved benches, spikes along brick windowsills (with retractable ones in front of doorways), rocky pavements in place of sandy paths, and other features for deterring the homeless. It also lists the costs involved, which range from thousands to millions of dollars. As NCH board member Bob Erlenbusch writes, "Given the proliferation of anti-homeless architecture, NCH can only surmise that the costs nationally are in the hundreds of millions of dollars—funds that could be used for emergency services and affordable housing."[20]

Declaring a State of Emergency

Initiatives to install so-called hostile architecture are just one example of laws specifically aimed at the homeless. Some of these laws are intended to help mentally ill homeless people. New York City mayor Eric Adams's 2023 mandate authorizes teams of outreach workers and police officers to move patients with severe mental illness to clinics or shelters for care. Other laws focus on reclaiming public spaces that have been occupied by the homeless. Some cities and states have passed measures to criminalize homelessness outright. Solutions that focus on the rights of the homeless often are met with a backlash from citizens more concerned about the safety and security of urban streets. Caught in the middle are chronic homeless cases, many with mental illness, who struggle to survive day after day with no fixed abode.

This conflict has played out in the city of Los Angeles, California. With its mild, sunny weather, Los Angeles has long been perceived as a haven for homeless people living outdoors. Its tent encampments extend for more than fifty blocks in the perilous Skid Row district east of downtown and the luxury high-rises of Bunker Hill. Thousands of homeless people exist in these makeshift shantytowns without utilities.

In September 2015 angry citizens were demanding action. Block after block was filled with drug users, mentally ill people languishing untreated, and lawless individuals looking to take advantage of helpless victims. Since 2013, when then-mayor Eric Garcetti had taken office, the number of homeless in Los Angeles

Some cities have started designing public benches with thick steel armrests in the middle to prevent homeless people from sleeping on them, like these benches in New York City.

had grown by 12 percent. The Los Angeles City Council declared a state of emergency on homelessness in the city and committed $100 million to address the mushrooming problem. Garcetti also announced plans to spend nearly $2 billion over the next decade to fund permanent low-cost housing. City officials hoped to ease restrictions on churches and nonprofit groups that provided emergency shelter for the homeless. They also planned to fast-track building permits for housing. "We all understand the urgency that this situation requires, and what is at stake," said Garcetti. "I applaud the Los Angeles City Council for their action today in earmarking a necessary initial investment that helps launch my comprehensive plan to tackle homelessness."[21]

Despite these measures, six years later the problem had grown much worse. Advocacy groups for the homeless sued the city, seeking relief for the Skid Row population. In April 2021, US district judge David O. Carter issued a scorching 110-page order that condemned the city's failed efforts to address the crisis. Carter ordered the city and county to find suitable shelter for all of Skid Row's homeless people, beginning with women and children, within 180 days. In his ruling for the advocacy groups,

Carter wrote, "All of the rhetoric, promises, plans, and budgeting cannot obscure the shameful reality of this crisis—that year after year, there are more homeless Angelenos, and year after year, more homeless Angelenos die on the streets."[22]

Carter's sweeping order was overturned on appeal, but the elderly judge conducted tours of Skid Row to draw attention to the issue, hugging homeless mothers and listening to pleas for help. By September 2023, the Los Angeles City Council was once more declaring a state of emergency on its unsolved homelessness problem. This time the council partnered with Los Angeles County to fund three thousand new beds for treatment of mental illness and substance abuse—a substantial jump from an earlier proposal of three hundred. Calling the new initiative a floor, not a ceiling, for improvements going forward, Carter praised the city's commitment. "This is an extraordinary step forward," he said. "It's going to save a lot of lives."[23]

> "All of the rhetoric, promises, plans, and budgeting cannot obscure the shameful reality of this crisis—that year after year, there are more homeless Angelenos, and year after year, more homeless Angelenos die on the streets."[22]
>
> —David O. Carter, US district judge

Frustration and Controversy in San Francisco

A January 2023 incident in front of an art gallery in San Francisco illustrated how public frustration with the homelessness problem can boil over. Owner Collier Gwin arrived early one morning to find a homeless woman camped outside his gallery. Not only had she spread her belongings on the sidewalk, but she also had defecated there. Exasperated at the mess, Gwin sprayed a garden hose on the sidewalk and at the woman. His actions, caught on a cellphone video, went viral at once, bringing outraged calls for his arrest. A few days later, the front glass door of Gwin's gallery was shattered. Another gallery was also vandalized, apparently by mistake.

Initially, Gwin showed little remorse. "She starts screaming belligerent things, spitting, yelling at me," he told interviewers. "At that point she was so out of control . . . I spray her with the hose and say, 'Move, move. I will help you.'"

Later, however, he apologized for his actions. Bay Area residents engaged in heated debates about the case, with many people agreeing with Gwin's contention that the city was broken. Ultimately, Gwin was convicted of misdemeanor battery and sentenced to thirty-five hours of community service.

Quoted in Tori Gaines, "SF Art Gallery Owner Filmed Spraying Homeless Woman with Hose Has Been Arrested," *The Hill*, January 19, 2023. www.thehill.com.

A Crucial Ruling on Homeless Rights

While cities like Los Angeles and San Francisco struggled to deal with the crisis, a landmark decision affecting the homeless and mentally ill promised to stir up even more controversy. In July 2018, the Ninth Circuit Court of Appeals ruled that homeless people could not be punished for sleeping outside on public property if no adequate alternatives were available. Essentially, the most powerful appeals court in the nation said that sleeping on city sidewalks had constitutional protection. It found that prosecuting people for such behavior is cruel and unusual punishment. The decision, which arose from a decade-old lawsuit in Boise, Idaho, bound nine western states, including California, to the same standard. Cities now had to provide shelter for unhoused people before they could begin making arrests and clearing their streets.

The ruling set off a storm of protests from cities, business owners, and private citizen groups. Dozens of cities filed legal briefs in support of Boise's position, which said that cities should be able to arrest homeless people even when no emergency shelter is available. City attorneys expressed fears that the circuit court's ruling was much too broad and could prevent enforcement of basic laws for health and safety. Meanwhile, as appeals worked their way through the courts, other cities searched for ways around the decision.

In 2022, the city of Phoenix, Arizona, cleared out its largest homeless encampment in response to another court order. Maricopa County Superior Court Judge Scott Blaney had ruled that the encampment constituted a public nuisance that subjected residential and commercial properties to litter, damage, and crime. More than one thousand unhoused people were evacuated from a fifteen-block area known as the Zone, where they had been living for several years. Sixteen outreach groups helped the city notify the Zone dwellers and prepare them for the move. The massive effort just managed to meet the court-ordered deadline. Most of the homeless were placed in temporary shelters, but some were taken to clinics for mental health care.

US district judge David O. Carter (left) talks with a former resident of Los Angeles's Skid Row to draw attention to the city's homeless problem. He has repeatedly condemned the city's failed efforts to address the crisis.

The following year, the city council in Portland, Oregon, outlawed camping on all public property between 8 a.m. and 8 p.m. The council also passed restrictions on where people can loiter during the rest of the day. However, a circuit court judge halted the ban four days before it was to take effect. Portland mayor Ted Wheeler was frustrated by the ruling, but he refused to give up on the issue. "I believe the status quo is not working, but the court's decision leaves the status quo in place," said Wheeler. "The city will abide by the court's preliminary order while continuing to fight in court for the city's right to adopt reasonable regulations on unsanctioned camping."[24]

In 2023, amid mounting protests from both cities and homeless advocates, the Ninth Circuit reaffirmed its 2018 ruling. Cities dealing with the aftermath of COVID-19 restrictions as well as swelling numbers of homeless people saw their residents' frustrations about to boil over. Legal experts pushed for some kind of resolution. After years of refusing to review the lower court's decision, the Supreme Court finally agreed to hear the case in its 2024 docket. Among those urging the court to act was California governor Gavin

Newsom. In a brief filed with the Supreme Court, Newsom described his concerns:

> While I agree with the basic principle that a city shouldn't criminalize homeless individuals for sleeping outside when they have nowhere else to go within that city's boundaries, courts continue to reach well beyond that narrow limit to block any number of reasonable efforts to protect homeless individuals and the broader public from the harms of uncontrolled encampments. It's time for the courts to stop these confusing, impractical and costly rulings that only serve to worsen this humanitarian crisis.[25]

Forcing the Mentally Ill into Treatment

Newsom took steps to deal with California's mentally ill homeless as well. In October 2023, the governor signed a new law that allowed for people with mental illness or drug addiction to be detained against their will and forced into treatment. The law redefined the term *gravely disabled* to include those who cannot provide for their own basic needs, including food and shelter. Previously, local officials had felt hamstrung in their efforts due to state law.

The new law also contained a reform of California's system of conservatorship, giving a court-appointed person more authority to make decisions for a person's care, such as receiving medical treatment and taking medications. It followed a new law passed the previous year that enabled families to petition a judge to create a treatment plan for people diagnosed with severe mental illness, such as bipolar disorder or schizophrenia. Mayors of some of the state's largest cities supported the reforms as the best method to get treatment for those with severe men-

> "The mental health crisis affects us all, and people who need the most help have been too often overlooked. We are working to ensure no one falls through the cracks, and that people get the help they need and the respect they deserve."[26]
>
> —Gavin Newsom, governor of California

Toward a National Homeless Bill of Rights

The National Law Center on Homelessness & Poverty has called for a national homeless bill of rights. It explains the need for such a law:

> Millions of homeless persons suffer violations of their civil and human rights on a routine basis. In response to this widespread discrimination, several states have enacted or proposed homeless bills of rights. These laws are designed to protect homeless people from common rights violations and, in some cases, to offer new, positive rights aimed at eliminating homelessness entirely. Homeless bills of rights have the potential to transform the legal landscape in America and to improve the lives of millions of homeless Americans. . . .
>
> The Law Center strongly supports homeless bills of rights, and works with state advocates to develop and promote them. We are hopeful that the growing trend toward utilizing this powerful legal tool will only continue to grow. . . . We encourage homeless advocates across the country to pursue these laws. . . . In addition, we urge legislators to pass these bills with clear and consistent declarations of support for the civil and human rights of homeless Americans. . . .
>
> In protecting the rights of our society's most vulnerable members, we also fortify and protect the rights of the majority. Only when equal treatment under the law is a reality for everyone can we truly be free.

National Law Center on Homelessness & Poverty, *From Wrongs to Rights: The Case for Homeless Bill of Rights Legislation*. Washington, DC: National Law Center on Homelessness & Poverty. https://homelesslaw.org.

tal health challenges. "California is undertaking a major overhaul of our mental health system," Newsom said at the signing event. "The mental health crisis affects us all, and people who need the most help have been too often overlooked. We are working to ensure no one falls through the cracks, and that people get the help they need and the respect they deserve."[26]

Pushing for a Homeless Bill of Rights

Many advocates for the homeless and mentally ill strongly oppose the new California laws. They also object to Mayor Adams's plan allowing forcible removal in New York. These critics see the use of force as a way to criminalize homelessness and dehumanize those who suffer with mental health problems. Moreover, they stress the trauma and other health dangers, including shortened life expectancy, that homeless people face when they are forcibly removed from their tent dwellings.

As cities and states resort to more extreme measures in their policies, advocacy groups see an increased need for a guarantee against government abuses. Some have proposed a homeless bill of rights that would codify the constitutional protections that homeless individuals and those with mental illness possess as citizens. The idea goes back at least a decade, when homelessness became such a large issue nationwide. In May 2023, New York City became the first city in the United States to pass a bill creating a homeless bill of rights. Supporters of the measure believe it offers robust legal protections for those living on the streets or in temporary shelters. It also affirms the right to sleep outdoors in public spaces—although certain areas remain off-limits. Some activists who support the bill also see the irony involved. "It's a sad state of affairs when we are basically asking, begging authorities to allow us to sleep in the elements," says Deborah Padgett, a leading expert on homelessness at New York University's Silver School of Social Work. "If you think about it, why should that be a right? Housing should be the right."[27]

Laws that address the mentally ill homeless have brought a variety of legal challenges across the nation. Advocates for the homeless seek to defend their rights and push for affordable housing, while businesses and citizen groups express concerns about public order and safety. It remains to be seen how this clash of viewpoints will affect policies on homelessness in the future.

> "It's a sad state of affairs when we are basically asking, begging authorities to allow us to sleep in the elements. If you think about it, why should that be a right? Housing should be the right."[27]
>
> —Deborah Padgett, a leading expert on homelessness at New York University's Silver School of Social Work

CHAPTER FOUR

Getting Necessary Medication

Kori was a smart, independent young woman with a loving family and a bright future in store. About fifteen years ago, however, her occasional dark periods began to descend into chronic mental illness. Kori would speak in odd accents and break out in fits of paranoia and anger. She was also drinking heavily, which convinced her family that the problem was alcohol related. After disappearing for weeks, Kori turned up in Vancouver, British Columbia, far from her home in Arizona. She had landed in a psychiatric hospital, where she was diagnosed with bipolar disorder. But she refused any treatment—a scenario that would play out repeatedly over the next six years. She ended up losing her husband, home, and savings. And her family, with no legal right to demand that she accept treatment, could only watch as her life fell apart.

Finally, Kori made threats on her father's life. This enabled her sister, Shannon, and other family members to get a court order mandating psychiatric treatment for her in their home state of Arizona. With medication, Kori's severe mental illness was brought under control. Seemingly herself again at age forty, she enrolled in community college and began planning again for the future. However, when the state's mandate for treatment expired after one year, Kori stopped taking her meds. She regressed immediately. Her behavior once more became unpredictable; she would lash out with threats and hateful rants.

For the last decade Kori has been living on the streets of Phoenix or Seattle, getting by on modest stipends from her

> "She won't tell me where she sleeps. . . . She won't work with mental health professionals or outreach programs. She runs at their mere mention."[28]
>
> —Shannon Miller, whose sister, Kori, is a homeless person with mental illness

parents. Occasionally, she stays in Shannon's home city of Menlo Park, California. "She won't tell me where she sleeps," says Shannon. "My family and I have tried to find out if she was eligible for disability or temporary housing, but we've made no real headway. She won't work with mental health professionals or outreach programs. She runs at their mere mention."[28]

The Right to Refuse Treatment

Kori's experience spotlights a key issue related to mental healthcare. Like many who suffer from serious mental illness, Kori is a radically different person depending on whether she has taken medication. Yet according to current law, she has a nearly absolute right to refuse treatment, even when her refusal seems certain to lead to trouble. Eventually, she was arrested for repeatedly threatening a person. Shannon desperately wants Kori to get psychiatric treatment, but instead her sister seems destined to spend months or years in jail.

Patients with mental illness like Kori's actually have both the right to treatment and the right to refuse it. Right-to-treatment laws developed alongside the push for quality-controlled public psychiatric hospitals. Such facilities must obtain certification to receive Medicare and Medicaid payments for care. A patient admitted to one of these certified hospitals has the legal right to receive the highest standard of psychiatric care.

Patients who voluntarily enter psychiatric hospitals—and show no signs of endangering themselves or others—may refuse treatment and demand to leave at any time. Yet even when patients are placed in psychiatric hospitals involuntarily, they still have the right to refuse treatment. Because of the possible danger to themselves or others, involuntary patients cannot leave the hospital until released by doctors. However, due to privacy rights, equal protection, and due process under the law, patients cannot be administered medications against their will. The only exception to this right of refusal comes when there is an emergency that presents an imminent danger to the patient or other people. The right of refusal remains in force whether a patient is in a hospital bed or a tent encampment on the streets.

The right of refusal is also based on the idea of informed consent. This means that patients understand five crucial things about their condition and possible treatment: the diagnosis, the proposed treatment, the risks and benefits of the treatment, possible alternative treatments with their risks and benefits, and the risks and benefits of declining treatment. Research indicates that even patients with severe mental illness, such as schizophrenia or bipolar disorder, can make informed decisions about their own care. Elyn Saks, a mental health expert and law professor at the University of Southern California, has written about her own bout with mental illness and the idea of informed consent. "Law is based

Patients who voluntarily enter psychiatric hospitals—and show no signs of endangering themselves or others—may refuse treatment and demand to leave at any time. Research indicates that even patients with severe mental illness, such as schizophrenia or bipolar disorder, can make informed decisions about their own care.

on a theory of personhood," Saks writes; "that is, the concept of someone who can make choices and suffer consequences. . . . The doctrine of informed consent (indeed, most of American political theory) presumes that we are not just subjects to be directed, but rather autonomous beings capable of making independent decisions."[29]

Dangers from Unmedicated Patients on the Streets

Some lawmakers and mental health experts fear that the right of refusal and informed consent are preventing people with severe mental illness from getting the treatment they need. There are also questions of public safety in cities with large homeless populations, such as New York, Los Angeles, and Portland, Oregon. Homeless people who fail to take necessary medications to control their mental illness can present a danger not only to themselves but also to other people on sidewalks and subways. Doctors who urgently want to provide psychiatric care find that

Why People with Mental Illness Refuse Medication

When homeless patients with mental illness refuse to take medication, caregivers may be frustrated but not surprised. Psychiatric professionals are used to seeing a number of common reasons why patients reject their meds. Perhaps the most common is the feeling that the medication does not work or is not needed. Drug treatment to counteract severe depression or schizophrenia often takes at least two to four weeks to deliver its full effect. If patients stop treatment in the middle, they may argue that the medication was not working anyway. Should their condition improve more quickly, they might insist there was no real problem to begin with.

There is also the stigma attached to mental illness and getting treatment for it. Patients come to view their condition as shameful and something to be denied. One of the best ways to convince patients to take meds is to gain their trust with shows of support, patience, and empathy. "We recommend that the prescribers talk to patients about their thoughts and experiences of the medications they take," says Asta Ratna Prajapati, a researcher at Brigham and Women's Hospital in Boston, "paying particular attention to these issues which may stop patients taking their meds."

Quoted in Tanetta Hassell, "Why Do People with SMI Like Bipolar Disorder or Schizophrenia Stop Taking Their Meds?," Western Tidewater Community Services Board, October 17, 2023. www.wtcsb.org.

their hands are tied by current laws and practices. "We are doctors who have to watch these people die," says psychiatrist Emily Wood, chair of the Government Affairs Committee of the California State Association of Psychiatrists. "We have to talk to their families who know that they need that care, and we have to say we don't have any legal basis to bring them into the hospital right now."[30]

> "We are doctors who have to watch these people die. We have to talk to their families who know that they need that care, and we have to say we don't have any legal basis to bring them into the hospital right now."[30]
>
> —Emily Wood, a psychiatrist and chair of the Government Affairs Committee of the California State Association of Psychiatrists

Statistics show the dimensions of the problem. A snapshot study of one night in 2023 by the National Alliance to End Homelessness revealed that about 31 percent of the homeless had severe mental illness. Another 24 percent were struggling with chronic substance abuse. Whereas only about 1 percent of the general public has schizophrenia, research indicates that it affects a staggering 20 percent of the homeless population. A 2019 study revealed that among patients who live mostly on the streets, 63 percent failed to take medications to control their mental illness. Among patients in stable housing, only 18 percent neglected to take necessary meds.

Tragedy Due to the Failure to Take Meds

A person's failure to take meds while living on the streets can end in tragedy. On January 15, 2022, a homeless man in Manhattan shoved a woman into the path of an oncoming subway train as she waited on the crowded platform of the Times Square station. The woman, forty-year-old Michelle Go, died at the scene. Just minutes before the attack on Go, the assailant, sixty-one-year-old Martial Simon, had randomly punched another waiting passenger, breaking the man's jaw. It transpired that Simon, who suffered from schizophrenia, had spent time in prison, jails, hospitals, and outpatient psychiatric programs for more than twenty years. With no regular access to long-term care, he had taken medication for his mental illness only sporadically.

A makeshift memorial seen at a candlelight vigil in Times Square for Michelle Go. Go was killed when a schizophrenic homeless man pushed her into an oncoming subway train in Manhattan.

Advocates for the homeless and mentally ill noted how the system had failed Simon. But others, pointing to Simon's history of violence and erratic behavior, questioned why he was still on the streets. People who knew Simon attested to his angry outbursts, although most of them did not think he was violent. In police custody, Simon admitted to pushing Go onto the tracks. He was charged with second-degree murder; however, he later was found unfit to stand trial and instead was sent to a psychiatric hospital for treatment. The *New York Post* Editorial Board demanded some accountability for Go's murder:

> Perhaps Simon's mental-health issues render him not technically responsible for his heinous deed. Yet *someone* should be held responsible for failing to provide sufficient care and oversight for people like him. Simon often complained that facilities were releasing him before he was stabilized. In 2017, he reportedly told a hospital psychiatrist it was only a matter of time before he shoved a woman onto the tracks—but he was released anyway.[31]

The editorial ended with a quote from Simon's sister, Josette: "To know my brother cost somebody their life, not because he's a bad person, but because he didn't get help? It's unbearable."[32]

Rising Tensions

Incidents like Go's death have raised tensions around the country about the possible threat from mentally unstable homeless people. Although mental health experts insist that people like Simon are mostly a danger to themselves and are more likely to become victims of violence than perpetrators, many remained unconvinced. Residents of New York became even warier of loud strangers in the subway and tried to keep their distance from the tracks until the train had arrived.

On May 1, 2023, another tragedy unfolded in the Manhattan subway. A thirty-year-old homeless man named Jordan Neely died in the chokehold grip of Daniel Penny, a twenty-four-year-old former

Breakdowns in Kendra's Law

In 2023, when Martial Simon killed Michelle Go in the Times Square subway, older New Yorkers were reminded of a similar incident more than twenty years before. In January 1999, Andrew Goldstein had shoved a thirty-two-year-old journalist named Kendra Webdale into the path of an oncoming subway train, killing her instantly. Goldstein was found to have suffered for years with schizophrenia. Although he had been sent to psychiatric centers for treatment, his stays were brief. Tabloid coverage of the incident brought calls for the state to act.

The result was passage of a bill dubbed Kendra's Law. It allowed for court orders to mandate a monitored treatment plan for people suffering from severe mental illness. Patients who broke from their plan could be hospitalized and required to take medication.

Following Go's death, the *New York Times* undertook a detailed analysis of whether Kendra's Law was working. The results were startling. People subject to strict monitoring under the law had committed more than 380 violent acts during the preceding five years, including beatings and stabbings. Five people subject to court orders had shoved strangers onto the subway tracks. As one patient's mother wrote to the State Office of Mental Health, "Once again he is falling through the cracks."

Quoted in Amy Julia Harris and Jan Ransom, "Audit Finds Fatal Lapses in Mental Health Program Meant to Curb Violence," *New York Times*, February 8, 2024. www.nytimes.com.

Marine. Neely, a street performer with a history of mental illness, had been screaming at passengers that he was hungry and thirsty and did not care if he died. Some witnesses admitted later that they felt threatened by Neely's behavior before Penny intervened. Amid protests and growing calls for his arrest, Penny was finally charged with second-degree manslaughter in the case. Some commuters who had encountered disorderly homeless people on the streets or subways felt conflicted about Penny's indictment.

Neely's story showed how a person diagnosed with severe mental problems could easily fall through the cracks of New York City's system of social welfare. Neely was fourteen when his stepfather murdered his mother. Relatives say he became clinically depressed and also suffered from PTSD, autism, and schizophrenia. He landed in New York's foster care system, but he aged out automatically when he turned twenty-one. He made pocket money by performing dance routines on the streets and in the subways. In constant brushes with the police, Neely claimed to be hearing voices and needing medication to control his jumbled

Protesters call for justice for a homeless man named Jordan Neely. Neely died in the New York City subway from the chokehold grip of a man who was subduing him after he threatened passengers.

thoughts. During the last decade of his life, Neely was arrested more than forty times for various offenses, including drug use, theft, and three assaults on women.

Rejecting Aid from Street Teams

While living on the streets, Neely also had several visits from intensive mobile treatment (IMT) teams offering physical exams and medication. However, he often refused psychiatric treatment or pretended not to need the meds that could control his schizophrenia. "If somebody is not in agreement with what a third party says their mental health treatment is going to be, they're very unlikely to continue following it independently," says Beth Diesch, who directs the homeless mobile teams for the nonprofit Community Access in New York City. "If a doctor says 'take this pill' and you don't think you need it, you're not going to do it."[33]

> "If somebody is not in agreement with what a third party says their mental health treatment is going to be, they're very unlikely to continue following it independently. If a doctor says 'take this pill' and you don't think you need it, you're not going to do it."[34]
>
> —Beth Diesch, homeless mobile team director for the nonprofit Community Access in New York City

In 2021, after he punched an elderly woman in the head, Neely was jailed on Rikers Island for second-degree assault. Released as part of a plea deal, he was supposed to live in an intensive inpatient treatment center for fifteen months. Instead, after less than two weeks, he managed to slip away. Neely proceeded to spiral further downward. Without medication, his angry outbursts increasingly erupted without warning, making confrontation more likely. "If there is a mental illness highway, and at the end of that highway is jail or prison, we need as many off-ramps from that highway as possible, so that people who are living with mental illness have opportunities to get help instead of handcuffs," says Matt Kudish, head of the National Alliance on Mental Illness of New York City. "It's not to say that the people who were working in these different [separated] systems didn't care about [Neely], but at some point, their role ends. Jordan needed someone on Jordan's side."[34]

CHAPTER FIVE

Working Toward Solutions

Eight years of life on the streets of San Francisco had left one twenty-four-year-old woman desperate for help. She had left home as a teenager, fleeing domestic violence and grinding poverty. Now she was homeless, filthy, suffering from delusions, and hooked on methamphetamines. In addition, she had somehow sustained such a serious infection in one hand that amputation seemed necessary. Fearful of going to a clinic, the woman had run out of options.

However, her fortunes took a positive turn with the arrival of a street psychiatry team led by an emergency physician named Aislinn Bird. The team, part of a Bay Area group called the Alameda County Health Care for the Homeless, noticed the young woman while roving through areas where the homeless congregated—under bridges, in ATM enclosures, and in tent encampments. Bird approached the young woman, asked her a series of questions as part of a psychiatric intake, and was able to diagnose her schizophrenia. After a number of visits, Bird gained the woman's trust. She administered a long-acting antipsychotic medication pulled from a medicine kit in her backpack. Further meetings with a psychiatrist and a primary care doctor convinced the woman to also take antibiotics for her hand. Soon the woman's infection had healed and her mental health was showing improvement. She was able to enter temporary transitional housing, where she could take regular showers and wean herself away from meth. Bird reported after their last visit that the young woman was calm, healthy, and working on her art.

Bringing Psychiatric Care to the Homeless

A persistent problem for homeless people with mental illness is their lack of access to health care. In fact, their homelessness is often the by-product of failure to obtain and take the medications they need to control their condition. Street psychiatry teams, like Bird's in the San Francisco Bay Area, strive to provide enough transitional care, including meds, to get people off the streets. "These are folks who may not have insurance or transportation or are too symptomatic or disorganized from their mental illness to think clearly enough to obtain care," says Dawn-Christi Bruijnzeel, an associate professor of psychiatry and founder of a street psychiatry program at the University of Florida. The object of such programs, she says, is not long-term care on the street. "Rather it's to help these folks get to the point where they are back on their feet, ideally housed, so that they can obtain care from clinics going forward. That initial care on the street is critical though because it enables them to relaunch their lives."[35]

> "[Street psychiatry teams] help these folks get to the point where they are back on their feet, ideally housed, so that they can obtain care from clinics going forward."[35]
>
> —Dawn-Christi Bruijnzeel, an associate professor of psychiatry and founder of a street psychiatry program at the University of Florida

Locating patients who need help and providing them with the medications they need calls for dedicated street-level efforts with plenty of follow-up checks. But street psychiatry teams like Bird's are being deployed in cities across the nation. The idea began about twenty years ago, as homelessness began to enter the national consciousness. It grew as hospitals realized that investing in street psychiatry could save money that would otherwise be spent on emergency care for the uninsured homeless. In 2017, the Lehigh Valley Health Network (LVHN) in Pennsylvania created teams that treated more than fifteen hundred homeless patients on the streets. The reduced number of emergency room visits and hospital admissions saved the LVHN an estimated $3.7 million for the year. Hospital networks in other states have achieved similar results. "[The homeless] often receive care for physical ailments in one of the highest-cost areas of the hospital, the emergency department," says Bruijnzeel. "If we're able to get people mentally healthier, then their physical health will improve, and it will decrease costs to the hospital system."[36]

Paying for Street Teams' Medical Care

A new initiative from the federal government is likely to help with budgeting problems. The Biden administration introduced a groundbreaking administrative change to support street medicine providers, including psychiatric teams. On October 1, 2023, the Centers for Medicare & Medicaid Services began to allow insurers, both public and private, to pay street medicine teams for the medical care they deliver to homeless people, regardless of the location. In the past, insurers would pay only for services delivered in hospitals and clinics. "It's a game-changer," says Valerie Arkoosh, secretary of Pennsylvania's Department of Human Services. "Before, this was really all done on a volunteer basis. We

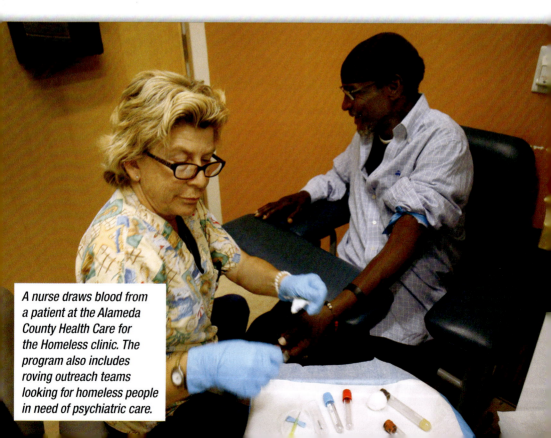

A nurse draws blood from a patient at the Alameda County Health Care for the Homeless clinic. The program also includes roving outreach teams looking for homeless people in need of psychiatric care.

Caring for the "Rough Sleepers"

Today's psychiatric care teams draw upon the innovations of an outreach pioneer in Boston. Dr. Jim O'Connell, an internist, has been leading his own operation, the Boston Health Care for the Homeless Program, for more than three decades. From its modest beginnings, the program grew to include more than four hundred workers and provided care for up to eleven thousand homeless people each year in South Boston—the "rough sleepers," as O'Connell calls them, using a common British expression. O'Connell and his crew navigate the streets of South Boston in one of two well-stocked vans, checking on those most in need of urgent care.

O'Connell's gift for outreach starts with his empathy and common touch. The Harvard graduate speaks easily with the people he approaches on the street. He is ready with a stethoscope, a blood pressure cuff, and meds if needed. One of his regulars, addled with delusions or drink, takes a few moments to recognize "Dr. Jim." But when he does, he is happy to see him and has plenty to say. He reminisces about some long-ago boozy adventures. O'Connell laughs and reminds him about the street clinic at Massachusetts General Hospital on Thursdays. As O'Connell admits, the secret to helping people is communication. "You have to learn to listen," he says.

Quoted in Tracy Kidder, "'You Have to Learn to Listen': How a Doctor Cares for Boston's Homeless," *New York Times,* January 5, 2023. www.nytimes.com.

are so excited. Instead of a doctor's office, routine medical treatments and preventive care can now be done wherever unhoused people are."[37]

However, not all places have found the same success with street psychiatry. New York City's IMT program aims to provide medications and psychiatric treatment to hundreds of the city's mentally ill homeless while also directing them to housing opportunities. But auditors have discovered that less than a third of IMT patients take their medications regularly. One-fourth of those in urgent need of treatment have never met with a nurse or psychiatrist from a street team. Critics say much of the $37 million spent on the program has been wasted. "We need the I.M.T. program to work—to help mentally ill and homeless New Yorkers get the treatment they urgently need," says Brad Lander, the comptroller who manages the program's funding. "Unfortunately, poor management and coordination mean the program

The Biden administration introduced legislation to support street medicine providers. The change allows insurers to pay street medicine teams for the care they deliver to homeless people on the streets.

is increasingly failing to help participants get off the street into stable housing—and we don't know whether or not it's working to keep I.M.T. clients and other New Yorkers safe."[38]

Prioritizing Housing with Housing First

Traditionally, in dealing with homelessness, it was thought essential to first treat homeless people's mental illness and wean them off drugs and alcohol. Once enrolled in a treatment program, they could then work toward becoming candidates for independent housing. But a different method of ending homelessness has now become the standard endorsed by most health care experts. Housing First, as its name suggests, focuses first on moving homeless people into permanent housing, even before attending to their mental illness or problems with substance abuse. The principle underlying Housing First is that people have a better chance of improving their chaotic lives if they first have a stable home. This holds true for the mentally ill as well as for anyone else. Once long-term housing is provided, support efforts can turn to other needs: physical and mental health, addiction counseling, education, and employment.

The idea behind Housing First originated during the 1990s, based on research by a New York psychologist and social worker named Sam Tsemberis. Working through his nonprofit group Pathways to Housing, Tsemberis was guided by his belief that housing is a basic human right. Making housing dependent on a person's behavior change seemed backward to him. And in his practice, he saw the results of such requirements. As Tsemberis recalls, he treated people during the day at Bellevue Psychiatric Hospital, then saw the same people on the streets on his way home.

He created Housing First to train groups on how to implement his model. He also conducted research on its results. As Housing First spread across the nation, reports showed that it produced higher success rates for housing the homeless than past approaches. Tsemberis won endorsements from the National Institutes of Health and the National Alliance to End Homelessness. In

A Promising Tool for Street Psychiatric Teams

Street psychiatric teams say patients often reject offers of housing due to paranoid delusions beyond their control. When informed about an opening in a local Los Angeles shelter, one street dweller declined the offer because he was certain that the building was a Mafia hideout and that there were twenty murders there almost every day. As street psychiatrist Brian Benjamin notes, "I do think there's a lot of times where there's a direct connection between their (homeless individuals') mental illness and their inability or unwillingness to go into housing."

Street teams like Benjamin's have faced a constant challenge getting these patients to keep up with their medications. But now a new medical tool shows promise for solving this problem. Mental health professionals like Benjamin can inject patients with a shot that provides a steady dose of antipsychotic medication that lasts a month or more. The shot is called Invega Sustenna, and it can be administered to treat schizophrenia, bipolar disorder, and other forms of severe mental illness. Its time-release feature aids patients who have struggled to make regular visits to treatment clinics or cannot remember to take daily meds. Benjamin is succinct about Invega's impact: "I think it's been a fundamental game changer."

Quoted in Clara Harter and Steve Scauzillo, "LA Is Losing the Battle Against Mental Illness Among Its Homeless," *Los Angeles Daily News,* January 28, 2023. www.dailynews.com.

New York social worker Sam Tsemberis (pictured) developed the research that was the basis for the Housing First program. The research was guided by his belief that housing is a basic human right.

2004, President George W. Bush made Housing First a key part of his administration's policy toward the mentally ill and homeless. "If we've demonstrated anything in the research that Housing First has shown," said Tsemberis, "it is that whether you are on board with harm reduction or giving people second, third or fourth chances or working from a compassionate point of view or not, we know it's actually very, very effective."[39]

Struggling with a Lack of Affordable Housing

In the last decade, Tsemberis's Housing First idea has become the default method for obtaining housing for the homeless mentally ill. The approach is based on a few bedrock principles. First, housing is provided with no preconditions. People do not have to pass a mental or physical examination, prove their sobriety, or give evidence of employment. Second, the name of the program may be Housing First, but it does not provide housing only. A variety of support services are made available, including treatment for mental health and substance use disorder. Third, people in Housing First are deemed to be ready for independent living. They are placed

> "If we've demonstrated anything in the research that Housing First has shown, it is that whether you are on board with harm reduction or giving people second, third or fourth chances or working from a compassionate point of view or not, we know it's actually very, very effective."[39]
>
> —Sam Tsemberis, a psychologist and social worker who created Housing First

into housing quickly, without time spent in transitional shelters or institutions. They are free to make choices about their own lives. Dwellings are generally small- to medium-size apartments, which are equipped with simple furnishings. Residents even pay rent in small amounts if they are able to secure employment.

Governments at all levels have made huge commitments to Housing First initiatives. Between 2018 and 2022, California spent $17.5 billion in its battle against homelessness, much of it devoted to Housing First programs. In January 2024, the Biden administration announced $3.16 billion in funding for seven thousand Housing First projects nationwide. Supporters point to decades of research showing that the approach is effective in getting homeless individuals housed and on the road to recovery. "Providing a safe, secure roof overhead immediately, then addressing other social service needs, is the most humane response to the needs of . . . the unhoused," says Fran Quigley, director of the Health and Human Rights Clinic at Indiana University. "It is also the most effective response, as Housing First's success in venues from Houston to Helsinki shows. Housing First sharply reduces the number of people who are unhoused and cuts the high cost of government interventions connected to homelessness."[40] But opponents claim that Housing First has been a disaster at cutting costs. They point to the billions that California and other states have spent on Housing First programs only to see their homeless numbers increase.

Moreover, say the opponents, California could have used the $17.5 billion it has spent on four years of Housing First to pay the rent for every homeless person in the state for that period.

Both sides of the debate acknowledge that a large part of the problem is the lack of affordable housing. Housing First advocates see the high price of buying or renting a home as the driving force behind the homelessness crisis and the crisis of the mentally ill. People who could lead stable lives when housing is available at a reasonable cost can suddenly find themselves on the streets when home prices soar. "We need 2.5 million more units in California," says Jason Elliott, a senior adviser to Governor Newsom on homelessness. "This is a problem that is decades and decades in the making because of policy choices that we've made. We are not blameless. And when I say we, I mean Republicans and Democrats alike."[41]

> "We need 2.5 million more [housing] units in California. This is a problem that is decades and decades in the making because of policy choices that we've made."[41]
>
> —Jason Elliott, a senior adviser to Governor Newsom on homelessness

Solutions to the problem of mentally ill people forced to live on the street have proved elusive. The effort to bring medical and psychiatric care to the urban homeless by way of mobile treatment groups has met with considerable success, but more such programs are needed. Housing First seeks to provide stable homes for those with mental illness, but its no-requirements approach and ballooning costs remain controversial. Going forward, urban planners and city officials will no doubt face more challenges as the numbers of the homeless mentally ill continue to grow.

SOURCE NOTES

Introduction: A Controversial Policy on the Mentally Ill Homeless

1. Quoted in CBS New York Team, "54 Mentally Ill New Yorkers Experiencing Homelessness Taken Off City Streets in Past Year, Mayor Eric Adams Says," CBS News, November 29, 2023. www.cbs.news.com.
2. Quoted in Jade Cobern and Nicole Wetsman, "Amount of Homeless People with Mental Illness Increased Slightly in Recent Years, but Experts Say They're More Visible: Analysis," ABC News, October 17, 2023. www.abcnews.go.com.
3. Quoted in Euan McKirdy and Mark Strassman, "Pioneering L.A. Program Seeks to Find and Help Homeless People with Mental Illness," CBS News, October 19, 2023. www.cbsnews.com.

Chapter One: A Problem with No Easy Solutions

4. Quoted in James Gordon, "How Star TV Journalist Became a Fantasist Who Lied to Alma Mater That She'd Donate $2M, Claimed She Was Friends with Prince Harry and Had Access to Private Jet . . . While She Was Sleeping in Parking Garage and Stealing Boxed Wine," Daily Mail, January 21, 2024. www.dailymail.co.uk.
5. Quoted in Gordon, "How Star TV Journalist Became a Fantasist Who Lied to Alma Mater That She'd Donate $2M, Claimed She Was Friends with Prince Harry and Had Access to Private Jet."
6. Quoted in Editorial Board, "The Solution to America's Mental Health Crisis Already Exists," New York Times, October 4, 2022. www.nytimes.com.
7. Divya Kakaiya, "Opinion: Here's How Reagan's Decision to Close Mental Institutions Led to the Homelessness Crisis," San Diego Union-Tribune, April 24, 2023. www.sandiegouniontribune.com.
8. Quoted in Rael Jean Isaac and D.J. Jaffe, "Toward Rational Commitment Laws: Committed to Help," Mental Illness Policy Org, January 23, 2019. https://mentalillnesspolicy.org.
9. Henry G. Cisneros, "The Lonely Death on My Doorstep," Washington Post, December 4, 1993. www.washingtonpost.com.

10. Melanie Fontes Rainer, "Commemorating the Olmstead Anniversary with Revitalized Enforcement Initiative," US Department of Health and Human Services, June 22, 2023. www.hhs.gov.
11. Harold I. Schwartz, "How We Are Failing Mentally Ill People," *New York Times,* February 15, 2022. www.nytimes.com.

Chapter Two: Challenges Faced by Mentally Ill Homeless People

12. Helping Hands Clinic, "Mental Illness for One Homeless Man." https://hhclinicgnv.org.
13. Quoted in Aaron Lai, "The 'Crushing' Cycle of Homelessness and Mental Illness," Breaktime, May 28, 2021. www.breaktime.org.
14. Quoted in Lai, "The 'Crushing' Cycle of Homelessness and Mental Illness."
15. Quoted in Rachel M. Cohen, "What a Landmark New Study on Homelessness Tells Us," Vox, July 5, 2023. www.vox.com.
16. Crisis Assistance Ministry, "The Cycle of Poverty and Mental Illness," October 10, 2023. www.crisisassistance.org.
17. Diana Grippo, "From Living on the Streets to a Career in High Tech," *Bipolar Chronicles* (blog), *Psychology Today,* April 9, 2021. www.psychologytoday.com.
18. Bethany Yeiser, "My Experience of Schizophrenia and Homelessness," *Recovery Road* (blog), *Psychology Today,* December 1, 2023. www.psychologytoday.com.
19. Quoted in Lai, "The 'Crushing' Cycle of Homelessness and Mental Illness."

Chapter Three: Laws Affecting Homeless People with Mental Illness

20. Bob Erlenbusch, *Design Against Humanity: Examining Anti-Homeless Architecture*. Washington, DC: National Coalition for the Homeless, 2023. https://nationalhomeless.org.
21. Quoted in Dana Ford, "Los Angeles Declares 'State of Emergency' on Homelessness," CNN, September 23, 2015. www.cnn.com.
22. Quoted in *The Guardian,* "Judge Orders Los Angeles to Shelter All Homeless Skid Row Residents," April 21, 2021. www.theguardian.com.
23. Quoted in Doug Smith, "Judge Approves L.A. County Deal for 3,000 Mental Health and Substance Use Treatment Beds," *Los Angeles Times,* September 29, 2023. www.latimes.com.

24. Quoted in Alex Zielinkski, "Judge Halts Enforcement of Portland's Camping Ban," *Oregon Public Broadcasting,* November 9, 2023. www.opb.org.
25. Quoted in Jeremy B. White, "Newsom Urges SCOTUS to Consider Encampment Ruling That Has 'Paralyzed' California Cities," *Politico,* September 22, 2023. www.politico.com.
26. Quoted in Olafimihan Oshin, "New California Law Could Force People with Mental Illness to Get Treatment," *The Hill,* October 11, 2023. www.thehill.com.
27. Quoted in Wilfred Chan, "Will America's First 'Right to Sleep Outside' Actually Help Unhoused People?," *The Guardian,* May 25, 2023. www.theguardian.com.

Chapter Four: Getting Necessary Medication

28. Shannon Miller, "My Sister Is Mentally Ill and Living on California's Streets. There's Nothing I Can Do to Help Her," *San Francisco Chronicle,* February 25, 2023. www.sfchronicle.com.
29. Quoted in Nathaniel Morris, "We Need to Rethink Mental Health Laws. But Not Because of Mass Shootings," *Washington Post,* March 2, 2018. www.washingtonpost.com.
30. Quoted in April Dembosky, Amelia Templeton, and Carrie Feibel, "State Lawmakers Eye Forced Treatment to Address Overlap in Homelessness and Mental Illness," KFF Health News, May 17, 2023. https://kffhealthnews.org.
31. Editorial Board, "If Michelle Go's Killer Is Unfit for Trial, Why Was He Free to Roam Streets in the First Place?," *New York Post,* April 20, 2022. www.nypost.com.
32. Quoted in Editorial Board, "If Michelle Go's Killer Is Unfit for Trial, Why Was He Free to Roam Streets in the First Place?"
33. Quoted in Wilfred Chan, "It's a Failure of the System: Before Jordan Neely Was Killed, He Was Discarded," *The Guardian,* May 12, 2023. www.theguardian.com.
34. Quoted in Chan, "It's a Failure of the System."

Chapter Five: Working Toward Solutions

35. Quoted in Linda M. Richmond, "Street Psychiatrists Build Trust, Offer Hope to Homeless Patients with SMI," Psychiatric News, March 17, 2023. https://psychnews.psychiatryonline.org.

36. Quoted in Richmond, "Street Psychiatrists Build Trust, Offer Hope to Homeless Patients with SMI."
37. Quoted in Angela Hart, "Health Care 'Game-Changer'? Feds Boost Care for Homeless Americans," California Healthline, October 18, 2023. https://californiahealthline.org.
38. Quoted in Jan Ransom and Amy Julia Harris, "New York Spends Millions on Mental Health Street Teams. Do They Work?," *New York Times,* February 7, 2024. www.nytimes.com.
39. Quoted in Joanne Zuhl, "Sam Tsemberis Has Revolutionized the Way We Think About Homelessness," *Street Roots,* November 11, 2020. www.streetroots.org.
40. Fran Quigley, "Housing First Is a Proven Solution to Homelessness in America," *The Hill,* September 10, 2023. www.thehill.com.
41. Quoted in Nick Watt, "California Has Spent Billions to Fight Homelessness. The Problem Has Gotten Worse," CNN, July 11, 2023. www.cnn.com.

FOR FURTHER RESEARCH

Books

Neil Gong, *Psychotics: Mental Illness and Homelessness in Los Angeles*. Chicago: University of Chicago Press, 2024.

Tracy Kidder, *Rough Sleepers.* New York: Random House, 2023.

Pat Morgan, *We Hardly Knew Them: How Homeless Mentally Ill People Became Collateral Damage.* Aurora, CO: Mile High, 2020.

Alisa Roth, *Insane: America's Criminal Treatment of Mental Illness.* New York: Basic Books, 2020.

Stephen B. Seager, *Street Crazy: America's Mental Health Tragedy.* La Quinta, CA: Westcom Associates, 2020.

Internet Sources

April Dembosky, Amelia Templeton, and Carrie Feibel, "State Lawmakers Eye Forced Treatment to Address Overlap in Homelessness and Mental Illness," KFF Health News, May 17, 2023. https://kffhealthnews.org.

Samuel Jackson, Kenneth Minkoff, and Stephanie LeMelle, "A Roadmap for Helping People Who Are Homeless and Mentally Ill," *Psychology Today,* January 4, 2023. www.psychologytoday.com.

Euan McKirdy and Mark Strassman, "Pioneering L.A. Program Seeks to Find and Help Homeless People with Mental Illness," CBS News, October 19, 2023. www.cbsnews.com.

Jared Meyer and Mike Riggs, "Debate: Mentally Ill Homeless People Must Be Locked Up for Public Safety," *Reason,* May 2023. https://reason.com.

Jan Ransom and Amy Julia Harris, "New York Spends Millions on Mental Health Street Teams. Do They Work?," *New York Times,* February 7, 2024. www.nytimes.com.

Linda M. Richmond, "Street Psychiatrists Build Trust, Offer Hope to Homeless Patients with SMI," Psychiatric News, March 17, 2023. https://psychnews.psychiatryonline.org.

Organizations and Websites

American Psychiatric Association (APA)
www.psychiatry.org
The APA promotes universal access to the highest quality of care for all people affected by mental disorders, including substance abuse disorders. The APA seeks to improve access to and the quality of psychiatric services to all patients, including the homeless.

Brookings Institution
www.brookings.edu
The Brookings Institution is a nonprofit organization whose mission is to conduct in-depth, nonpartisan research to improve policy and governance at local, national, and global levels. Its website includes several reports on the link between mental illness and homelessness, including *3 Social Triggers for Behavioral Health Needs—and What to Do About Them*.

Mental Health America
https://mhanational.org
Mental Health America is a national nonprofit that promotes mental health, well-being, and illness prevention. Its annual *State of Mental Health in America* report is among the most widely respected health reports in the nation. Its website includes articles on mental illness and homelessness, such as "3 Tips If You're Facing Housing Insecurity."

National Alliance to End Homelessness
https://endhomelessness.org
The National Alliance to End Homelessness is a nonpartisan, nonprofit organization committed to preventing and ending homelessness in the United States. Its website features an analysis of Housing First, the homeless assistance approach that prioritizes providing permanent housing for people who are homeless.

Pathways Housing First Institute
www.pathwayshousingfirst.org
As developers of the Housing First model, the Pathways Housing First Institute is the premier source for training, implementation, assessment, and research for this innovative approach. The institute stresses the right of people to have immediate access to housing without mental health treatment or sobriety tests.

Substance Abuse and Mental Health Services Administration (SAMHSA)
www.samhsa.gov

SAMHSA is one of the leading federal agencies addressing the issue of stable housing for individuals with serious mental illness. SAMHSA funds several key programs aimed at assisting individuals experiencing homelessness. Its website includes reports and data on homeless people who suffer from severe mental illness.

INDEX

Note: Boldface page numbers indicate illustrations.

Adams, Eric, 4, 5, 29
Adams, Yetta, 14–15
American Civil Liberties Union (ACLU), 13
American Psychiatric Association (APA), 9, 60
American Sociological Review (journal), 7
Americans with Disabilities Act (1990), 15
Arkoosh, Valerie, 48–49

Biden, Joe/Biden Administration, 16, **50**
   efforts to support street medicine by, 48
   Housing First projects and, 53
bipolar disorder, 24
Bird, Aislinn, 46
Blaney, Scott, 32
Bruijnzeel, Dawn-Christi, 47–48
Bush, George W., 15, 52

California Statewide Study of People Experiencing Homelessness (CASPEH), 22, 23
Carter, David O., 30–31, **33**
Cisneros, Henry G., 14
Community Mental Health Centers Act (1963), 11
conservatorship, 34
Crisis Assistance Ministry (Charlotte, NC), 24
Curtis, Lois, 14

deinstitutionalization, 11–12
   Medicaid passage and, 10
   as primary cause of rise in homelessness, 13
Department of Housing and Urban Development, US (HUD), 5
Design Against Humanity (National Coalition for the Homeless), 28–29
Diesch, Beth, 45

Elliott, Jason, 54
employment, challenge to the homeless in finding, 21
Ennis, Bruce, 13
Erlenbusch, Bob, 29

Food, Drug, and Insecticide Administration, US, 10
forcible removal, 4, 7
Franklin, Jo, 8–9

Garcetti, Eric, 29, 30
Go, Michelle, 41, 43
   memorial for, **42**
Goldstein, Andrew, 43
Government Hospital for the Insane (Washington, DC), **10**
Grippo, Diana, 24–25
Gwin, Collier, 31

Helping Hands Clinic (HHC, Gainesville, FL), 18, 19
homeless bill of rights, 35, 36
homelessness
   associated with trauma, 26
   criminalization of, 29
   daily challenges of, 19–21
   deinstitutionalization as primary cause of rise in, 13
   as trigger for mental disorders, 19
   vicious cycle of, 21–23
homeless population, 5

prevalence of mental disorders among, 17
hostile architecture, 28–29
housing, affordable
   advocacy for, 36
   lack of, 4, 21, 52–54
   spending on anti-homeless architecture *vs.*, 29
Housing First projects, 50–54

Insane: America's Criminal Treatment of Mental Illness (Roth), 11

Jamieson, Sue, 14

Kakaiya, Divya, 13
Kendra's Law, 43
Kudish, Matt, 45
Kushel, Margot, 23

Los Angeles
   homeless encampments in, **25**, 29–30
   homeless outreach in, 7
   increase in treatment beds in, 31

Medicaid, 10
   coverage of mobile treatment teams by, 48
   funding of mental health services has been inadequate, 16
medication(s)
   reasons people refuse, 40
   right to refuse, 38–39
mental disorders
   percentage of prison inmates suffering from, 11
   poverty as trigger for, 23–24
   prevalence of, among homeless population, 17
   state of being homeless as trigger for, 19
   See also treatment/therapy
Mental Health America, 60

mental health treatment. *See* treatment/therapy
mental hospitals
   federal, end of funding for, 12
   state, drop in patients living in, 11
mental illness, prevalence among homeless population, 5
Miller, Shannon, 38

National Alliance to End Homelessness, 41, 60
National Association of Mental Illness (NAMI), 23, 24
National Coalition for the Homeless (NCH), 28–29
National Law Center on Homelessness & Poverty, 35
Neely, Jordan, 43–45
   protest over death of, **44**
New Freedom Initiative (G.W. Bush administration), 15
Newsom, Gavin, 33–34, 35, 54
New York City
   efforts to address homelessness in, 4–5
   intensive mobile treatment in, 45, 49
New York Post (newspaper), 42–43
New York Times (newspaper), 43

Olmstead v. LC (1999), struggles to implement goals of, 14, 15
One Flew Over the Cuckoo's Nest (film), 12
   scene from, **12**
opinion polls. *See* surveys

Padgett, Deborah, 36
Pathways Housing First Institute, 60
Penny, Daniel, 43–44
Phoenix, AZ, clearing out of homeless encampments in, 32
polls. *See* surveys

Portland, OR, restrictions on homeless in, 33
post-traumatic stress disorder (PTSD), 26
Prajapati, Asta Ratna, 40
Price School of Public Policy (University of Southern California), 20
prison inmates, percentage receiving counseling/therapy, 11
Psychiatric Times (journal), 19

Quigley, Fran, 53

Rab, Shayan, 7
Rainer, Melanie Fontes, 16
Reagan, Ronald, 12
Roth, Alisa, 11

Saks, Elyn, 39–40
San Francisco, frustration with homeless in, 31
schizophrenia, 14, 21, 24, 26
  among deinstitutionalized population, 12
  conservatorship and, 34
  informed consent and, 39
  treatment of, 10, 11
  untreated, dangers of, 15
Schwartz, Harold I., 17
Sharfstein, Steven, 9
Simon, Martial, 41–42, 43
Smith, Janet, 19, 21, 27
street medicine/mobile treatment teams, 45, 54
  federal payment for, 48–49
substance abuse, percentage of homeless dealing with, 41
Substance Abuse and Mental Health Services Administration (SAMHSA), 61

suicide, 19
Supreme Court, ruling on disability rights, 14
Survey of Prison Inmates, 11
surveys
  on homeless population/mental health issues among, 17
  of prison inmates, on mental health/ treatment, 11

Thorazine, 10, 11
transportation, lack of, 19–20
treatment/therapy
  laws forcing homeless into, 34–35
  mobile, 45, 48–49, 54
  percentage of prison inmates receiving, 11
  right to refuse, 38–40
Trout, Hugh, 8–9
Tsemberis, Sam, 51, 52, **52**, 53

University of California, San Francisco (UCSF), 5

violence
  domestic, homelessness caused by, 26, 46
  homeless people more likely to become victims of, 43
  by mentally ill, 41–42

Webdale, Kendra, 43
Wheeler, Ted, 33
Williams, Julie, 26
Wilson, Elaine, 14
Wood, Emily, 41

Year of Community Living program (Obama administration), 15
Yeiser, Bethany, 26–27